Friends and Gems Freedom

Life Changing Bible Studies and Cooking Workshops

By

Bonnie McPhail

15 14 13 12 11 10 09 08   8 7 6 5 4 3 2 1

Friends and Gems Freedom

Life Changing Bible Studies and Cooking Workshops

ISBN-13: 978-1468181562 ISBN-10: 1468181564

It would be an absolute honor for you to include us in your new book. I am thrilled about the character being named after us. You are too kind. Things here at Chandler are going great. Our ladies had lots of positive comments from the service you were with us, you were truly a blessing. Thanks again for your kind words and for thinking of us here at Chandler Assembly

Judy Martin
Pastor's Wife
Chandler First Assembly

My ladies really enjoyed the evening we spent with Bonnie McPhail. Not only did we learn to make elegant candles, soaps and lotions we also learned a little bit about ourselves and each other as we laughed together and enjoyed Bonnies sweet gentle spirit and creative teaching. Bonnie has a true gift for ministry and a way of making every lady feel special.

Jessica Ramirez
Women's Ministry Coordinator
New Life Center

My passion is coaching others to find their sweet spot, the place where their God-given talent and abilities takes flight in their own unique way. When Bonnie began publishing her writings, I was thrilled. Bonnie is an example to other women to rise up and start doing what God has been prompting.

The ideas and crafts will inspire you to grab some girlfriends and create beautiful gifts together, while being encouraged by the uplifting stories. I can sincerely say that everything Bonnie writes is from a heart full of Christ's love. Open your heart to receive these words of love, and be ready to take flight in your unique way!

-Kathy Key, Life Coach & Women's Ministries Leader

~Dedicated to~

The wonderful women at Chandler First Assembly in Chandler Oklahoma you have the distinction of being my very first. You welcomed me into your hearts and I will forever carry you in mine.

Introduction

Of all the books the Lord has given me to write this one feels the most important. I believe the heartbeat of the Lord is for all of us to live a life that sets us free to be the beautiful women that he created us to be.

Over the years I have seen many women including myself, battle with feelings of unworthiness, lack of purpose, hopelessness, insecurity, and fear of every sort. Some of it was the result of their own lack of experience or poor choices or unspeakable victimization at the hands of others. Fear from whatever the source is rampant in our society.

The picture on the cover is a cherished memento of the early years of my family. We look like an ordinary family with a mother, father and four children. I see the happy smiles and my parents were filled with the same hopes and dreams that every young couple experiences.

Little did they know that only a few short years after this picture was taken the ravages of alcoholism in our family would bring mental, physical and sexual abuse to each of their precious children perpetrated by drunken friends without their knowledge.

They could not know when this happy picture was taken that years on down the road there would be anger, fighting, infidelity and divorce and dreams smashed like shards of broken glass.

For myself I became insecure and ashamed. The beautiful gifts and abilities that God placed in me to be used for his purposes were hidden behind a curtain of fear; my own personal self-imposed shield around my heart.

For years I was the peacemaker and any sort of conflict would literally turn me inside out emotionally. I was afraid of the dark because I was molested in the dark. I was afraid to be who God created me to be for fear I would be rejected or misunderstood so I just kept it all inside and so I hid.

There have been several life changing events that have brought me to the place where I can be transparent and confidant enough to share this with you, the first was the day at age 16 when I accepted Jesus Christ as my Lord and Savior. That moment began the journey that would ultimately set me free.

The second was the amazing man that God gave me to be my husband who loved me unconditionally and was able to help me peel back the layers, and walk out from behind the walls I had built around my heart. God knew just what I needed and he graciously provided.

The same night I came to know the Lord so did my sister Ann. The difference in us was so profound that a few months later my father gave his heart to the Lord and his drinking stopped. It was an amazing beginning.

Over the years one by one each member of my family came to know the Lord and they are each walking out their own individual journey just like I had to.

At the end of my father's life he had all four of his children around his bedside. Forgiveness and love sent him off on his beautiful journey home to be with the Lord.

It has been years in the making and the journey has not always been easy but God has been so faithful.

I have learned along the way that God is waiting to help us and he will send us exactly the right people, the right circumstances, the perfect opportunities.

I haven't fully arrived yet and the older I get the more I understand that life is truly a process, step by step we go from glory to glory, but I am a living testament to the fact that God is faithful and nothing is impossible with him.

The three books in this set will be a valuable tool in your tool kit. *A One Year Bride* is a work of fiction but much of what the main character experiences in the book I too have personally experienced. The Lord gave me the entire book in a dream and then every day after that I would dream the chapters. He did a healing in me while he used me to write the book. We serve a WONDERFUL God!

The second book in the set is a journal called *Keeper of the Freedom*. I greatly encourage you to write your thoughts out as you go through this course. Even for those of you who have not discovered the amazing benefits of journaling and feel as if you don't know where to start. Journaling is a powerful tool. Write your thoughts, write your fears, write what you are thankful for, and your dreams. I promise you God will speak personally to you.

Friends and Gems Freedom is meant to be used in conjunction with the other two and there will be reading and writing assignments from both of the other books.

I am so EXCITED because I know God has a mighty plan for your life. Let's get started!

Freedom

By
Bonnie McPhail

I ride on the winds of the freedom of God.
Soaring above all the places I trod.
Encased in his love and kept in his care;
freedom from all that trapped me back there.

Table of Contents

Dear Friends

Welcome to *Friends and Gems Freedom*! This is the fourth book in the *Friends and Gems* series and is a set of three books, the set contains a journal called *Keeper of the Freedom* for you to record your own personal freedom journey, a work of fiction called *A One Year Bride*; many who have read it said they were not able to put it down until they read it cover to cover and *Friends and Gems Freedom* which contains life changing bible studies and cooking workshops. You can use all three books together or separately and they will make a wonderful addition to your library.

You will be learning wonderful truths that you can apply to your own life all the while enjoying fellowship and fun as you share your favorite recipes with your friends.

Food, fellowship AND fun! What could be better than that?

The book also contains an instructor's guide and can be done privately in your own home with your friends or for church groups.

At the end of each of the lessons there will be recipe to be shared with you. These are my own personal favorites. Each week be prepared to bring your favorite ones and share them. You can cook them together or put them in a book as a reminder of this very special time in your lives.

It is powerful when women get together and share their sorrows, joys, worry's and concerns and lift each other up. No one can encourage like your friends and they will bring their own "gems" to help you to freedom.

You are getting ready for a life changing event!

~ Week One ~

Excerpt from A One Year Bride

Chapter Two

It was a steamy hot day; with no air conditioning the house was beyond Megan's endurance. She rolled out of her crumpled bed drenched in sweat.

The lukewarm shower loosened her tense muscles. There was no hot water either because it was an electric hot water heater. *I will never take electricity for granted.*

She had been having the nightmares again. Images of her parents crushed, broken, bleeding bodies and Eric's face marred beyond recognition and drenched in blood. She couldn't shake the gruesome images out of her head.

They had all gone out to dinner to celebrate the new baby. She and Eric had tried for ten years to get pregnant. Wistful happy memories played in her mind.

"You look gorgeous." Eric's eyes were shining as he wrapped his arms around her and dropped a kiss on top of her head.

"I'm so happy Eric. The Lord has given me my biggest dream to be able to have your baby."

He slid his arm from her shoulders and softly caressed her belly. "I hope it's a girl." He whispered against her hair.

She looked into his eyes shimmering with unshed tears.

"We are so blessed." And he turned her around to give her a long sloppy kiss.

She giggled and pulled gently away. "Better stop that Casanova or we'll have to explain to my parent's why we were late."

He pulled her close and held her tight; it was as if he couldn't get enough of her. "The day the Lord brought you into my life was the best day of my life." He whispered.

"Come on handsome we have to go!" Her push was a little firmer this time. If they didn't stop they wouldn't even make it to the restaurant. They'd soon be having way to much fun getting lost in each other's love.

She turned around only to catch him staring after her with such love and a big goofy smile; her handsome prince charming. It wouldn't have taken much to stay home wrapped in his arms. She wished now she had done that maybe things would have not turned out the way they did.

They got into his small compact and strapped in their seatbelts. In just a few moments they arrived at their favorite restaurant. Her dad was standing outside waiting for them.

"Hi Daddy!"

"Hi Sugar."

His embrace was strong and familiar. He'd worn the same cologne since she was a little girl. The musky fragrance of *Old spice* was still her favorite.

The tall handsome man with the same emerald eyes and auburn hair as her own was Michael Anderson, Pastor Mike to everyone else in the small community church he pastored; but to Megan he would always be "Daddy."

"Oh Daddy, I miss you so." She choked back the sob with the memory. It was still so painful and so incredibly raw. As bad as it hurt she was determined to finish the remembering.

"Your Mom's right over here."

He walked in front of her leading the way. She turned around and winked at Eric who was following behind her for the special news they were about to share.

Her mother; Elizabeth Anderson, "Ellie" was a petite slender woman of just barely over five feet tall. Her only daughter and her husband both towered over her. Sun kissed blonde hair and crystal blue eyes were in sharp contrast to her husband and daughter's identical looks.

She reached out her arms to both Megan and Eric enveloping them in a love filled embrace. "How wonderful it is to see you both and get to spend some family time together."

Ellie was a perfect complement to her shy reserved husband; he always so reluctant to share his inner most thoughts with anyone but his family and closest friends. She on the other hand drew a crowd wherever she went, her easy laughter and natural way of putting other's at ease always endeared her to everyone. Ellie never met a stranger.

Megan was a combination of them both with her father's looks and her mother's personality, it was a stunning combination.

Eric didn't say much during the meal. His love and pride for his beautiful wife shone in his eyes. They sparkled with the treasure of the secret.

Megan blushed at the looks he was giving her, remembering the kiss earlier and where it was most likely going to lead as soon as he got her home.

After dessert Eric reached for her hand. "Mom, Dad we have an announcement." She could still feel the warmth of his strong fingers curled around her own.

Ellie and Mike sensing the excitement exchanged hopeful glances. Could this be it? The moment they had been waiting for these ten long years?

Eric reached into his pocket and pulled out a crumpled, blurry photograph placing it in the middle of the table. There was a picture of a pregnancy test the words "pregnant" clearly emblazed on it.

"Oh Megan!" Ellie clapped her hands over her mouth to stifle a squeal and tears ran unchecked down her face.

Mike sat with a stunned smile frozen on his face. "Praise God! We have waited so long for this moment." When he took out his hankie to wipe tears of his own there wasn't a dry eye around the table.

All too soon the beautiful meal was over. Megan remembered how they all talked over each other laughing and sharing fond memories of her childhood. She could still hear the quiet timber of her father's voice as he bowed his head and prayed a prayer of thanksgiving just before they left.

"Dear Lord, we rejoice in the new life you have given Megan and Eric. We pray that this new baby will be kept safe and that she will know you all the days of her life. We ask these things in the precious name of your son Jesus."

The prophetic prayer still made gooseflesh rise on her arms. How could he have possibly known the baby was to be a girl? It was a comforting thought that maybe the Lord gave him special insight just before he was to be taken home.

Tears ran unchecked now. "Why God? Why did you let this happen? I don't understand." A familiar scripture eased into the back of her mind. "My ways are higher than yours..." She was strangely comforted by the passage.

"I trust you Lord. I don't understand but I trust you." There it was that gentle sweet peace that went past her understanding.

Megan poured out her heart to God, all of her questions, doubts, worries and fears tumbled out in a long cry of her anguished soul and when she was done and the sobs subsided she felt hope arise in her heart and the knowing that somehow God was going to make a way for her. She didn't know how he was going to provide she just knew he would.

~Lesson One~

Freedom from Fear

"For God has not given us a Spirit of fear, but of power and of love and a sound mind."
2 Timothy 1:7 N.K.J.V.

In the previous story we read about Megan Anderson who has just tragically lost her mother, father and husband in an automobile accident. She has run out of money and is in a desperate life situation. If anyone has reason to fear she does.

I think at one time or other most of us have had something in our lives that has caused us to fear.

Make a list of the things you are afraid of:

_____

_____

_____

_____

_____

_____

_____

_____

_____

_____

_____

_____

_____

_____

Later when you have some quiet time write the answers to these questions in your journal and be prepared to choose one of the questions next week to share with the group.

1. Has there ever been a time in your life when you felt afraid?

2. Have you ever questioned God? Been angry with him? Wondered why?

3. Have you or someone you knew ever faced impossible odds? What happened?

4. What fears are you dealing with today?

5. Take a moment and close your eyes; while you are thinking about the thing you are afraid of what just popped into your head? Write what you saw.

Let's take a look at this familiar passage of scripture.

You can each takes turns reading a verse out loud together.

When you are finished reading share with each other

how the verses spoke to your heart.

"Hallelujah! It's a good thing to sing praise to our God;

praise is beautiful, praise is fitting.

God's the one who rebuilds Jerusalem, who regathers

Israels's scattered exiles.

He heals the heartbroken and bandages their wounds.

He counts the stars and assigns each a name.

Our Lord is great, with limitless strength; we'll never

comprehend what he knows and does.

God puts the fallen on their feet again and pushes the wicked into the ditch.

Sing to God a thanksgiving hymn, play music on your instruments to God,

Who fills the sky with clouds, preparing rain for the earth, then turning the mountains green with grass,

Feeding both cattle and crows

He's not impressed with horsepower; the size of our muscles means little to him.

Those who fear God get God's attention; they depend on his strength." Psalm 147:1-7 T.M.B

Prayer

Dear Lord,

This has been a precious time of sharing with each other about what we are afraid of. I thank you that we are beginning an amazing journey together. Thank you for what you have shown us today.

In each of our quiet time while we record our thoughts in our journals I ask that you bring freedom from fear. Set us free Lord that we may be vessels to bring you honor.

We give you praise in advance for all that you are going to do in us and through us.

Thank you Lord…

~Fear Not~

"I am with you in the storm.
I am with you in the valley.
I am with you during the most difficult
and challenging times of your life.
Fear not little one, I am with you.
I care deeply about the things that you care about.
Let me carry them.
Remember, I still the storm to a whisper..."
~ The Lord ~

Scripture

"Let not your heart be troubled, neither let it be afraid."
John 14:27 N.K.J.V.

(Angel Songs Volume III
Messages of Hope and Love)

~Hand Made Rolls~

Step One – Gather Supplies

Ingredients:

- ♥ 1 stick of melted butter
- ♥ 1 package of yeast
- ♥ 1/3 cup sugar
- ♥ ½ cup milk
- ♥ ½ cup water
- ♥ ½ tsp salt
- ♥ 1 egg
- ♥ 4 and ½ cups flour

Step Two

Mix all ingredients together. I usually put them in the bread maker and set it on the dough setting. Let rise for about an hour and a half.

Step Three

Preheat the oven to 350 degrees. Place a small amount of flour on the surface you will be working with for me it's generally the countertop. Place the dough on the floured surface and cut into four pieces and shape each into a ball.

Step Four

Flatten each ball and cut into four. They will be shaped like a triangle. Roll from the wide end to the small end to achieve the crescent shape of the rolls.

Step Five

Butter the bottom of your pan, place the rolls on the pan and bake at 350 degrees for about 20 – 25 minutes until golden brown.

A Note to the Instructor:

Welcome! You have been chosen as the instructor of this program to follow the prompting of the Lord and guide this group of women.

You will find it is well worth all of the extra time, effort, and, most importantly, prayer needed for each of the women in your group. This will be a very special time in their lives, as well as your own, and God has chosen YOU to lead it! Remember: Those He calls, He equips. So even if you have never done this before, He will help and guide you along the way.

To make things a bit easier for you (especially if this if your first time leading a group) I have chosen to include instructor guides with this study. They will be loaded with tips, how-to's, and suggested time parameters for each class to help you achieve the goals of each session and workshop.

One of the most important things to do with a new group is to establish yourself as the leader right away. This is the role the Lord has given you for this specific time and place, with this particular group of women. Even if they are long-time friends, there still needs to be order or chaos (though often fun!) will occur.

There are specific truths that the Lord wants to speak to these women—and to you—so it's important to keep the flow going. Believe me, the women will greatly respect you for maintaining order; it is the sign of a good leader. And good leaders make people feel safe.

There are some guidelines that MUST be followed if you want your group to be successful:

First, explain to the women right away that anything shared in confidence stays in the room. It is not to be shared with anyone else—not even to have others outside the room "pray about it." This needs to become a safe place for the women over the next several weeks. You will be amazed as you watch beautiful new friendships and special relationships emerge in these few short weeks. Women are relational by nature, and this is a perfect venue for that need to be met. So nurture it by having the group keep confidences.

Next, it is of the UTMOST importance that strict time parameters are observed. Generally, if the meeting is held at the church, there are other programs going on simultaneously, such as youth and children's ministries. It would not be safe for the kids to be running around the parking lot unsupervised while their mom is in a class that is running late. Not to mention, unfair to babysitters who have already given from their hearts and are ready to go home. Your pastor or women's ministry leader will likely give you more leadership opportunities down the road if you demonstrate that you can be mindful of the group's time—and not cave in to the demands of a few who might tend to dominate.

Also, set parameters on sharing "too much information." Often there will be needy, hurting women in your group who will want to "unload." While there's certainly a time and place for that, generally it's not in such a public setting. Oftentimes after someone shares too much, she feels badly for exposing her inner hurts. She may even choose not to return to the group because she feels awkward and uncomfortable.

If a woman needs to unburden herself, it's best to encourage her to set up a scheduled appointment with the pastor. After all, he has been called to be the shepherd of the flock. Or, he may be able to refer her to someone else who can help, if he feels that's more appropriate.

It will be important not to allow anyone to monopolize the conversation. Sometimes, in keeping with their various personalities, some women just love to be the center of attention. They may not even be aware of it. Your love and gentle guidance will help them greatly in this important area.

If we, as Christians, strive to put others' needs above our own, that sometimes means letting someone else have a turn to speak—even when we're dying to share our thoughts. It's all part of the process of learning to be servants and highly esteem others, seeking to meet their needs. There is such joy in doing this when we learn to put ourselves last. But it does take practice!

Be on the lookout for those women who are not participating and attempt to gently draw them into the discussion. Often these women have wonderful "gems" to share with their friends, but they may feel shy and uncomfortable. Remember: It is your job to take care of the needs of the group. Doing so makes the women feel valued—and that can give them enormous confidence. Your support may be the very thing that gives them boldness to confront their own shyness—and overcome their personal obstacles.

Finally, pray for your group of women. This is one of the most important things that you can do. Prayer can accomplish amazing things in these women's hearts—some you might not ever know about.

For this period of time, you have been specifically chosen to lead this particular group of women. I know you do not take that privilege lightly. It is a great honor!

Instructor's Guide Lesson One

The class and workshop will be structured for 1 hour and 15 minutes.

Welcome – 20 minutes

Introduce yourself to the group.

Have the women go around the room and introduce themselves.

Hand out sign-up sheets for food, if you choose to have food at the gatherings. Hand out the attendance sheet, which should include room to write email addresses, phone numbers and mailing addresses. You will want to assign someone in the group to call or email the women—especially if they miss a meeting. This is such an important outreach for them, and will truly makes them feel valued.

Hand out books for those who have purchased them (unless your group has decided to purchase them and give them away as an outreach).

Help them get familiarized with the book.

Lesson - 20 minutes

Break the women into small groups and have each group read the lesson, assign one of the questions from the bible lesson to each group. (The first lesson is purposefully short because there is so much to accomplish for the first time together). Have each group choose a team leader who will present to the group at large.

Let the women read the lesson and discuss the assigned question for about 10 minutes among themselves and be prepared to share.

Have the team leader read the answer to the question you gave them.

Women LOVE to share with each other and this give them the opportunity to do just that. It also keeps the flow of conversation going, and it also helps everyone to begin to feel comfortable with each other.

Recipe Share - 10 minutes

For the first meeting you might like to bring some of your own recipes and let the women choose from them or hand out blank recipe cards and they can copy and share from each other.

Lesson questions – 15 minutes

You can break the women into small groups or if this is a home group sit around the kitchen table together and choose questions to talk about.

Wrapping It Up and Prayer Time – 10 minutes

Let the women know it is time to end the class for the evening, and close in prayer.

~ Week Two ~

Excerpt From A One Year Bride

Chapter Seven

Megan woke up in the middle of the night startled and disoriented. It took a few moments for her to get her eyes adjusted to the strangeness of her new room.

James had obviously put a lot of thought into this space. He had chosen soft earth tones with touches of burgundy, greens and navy blues; all the same color pallet she had chosen in her own home.

He knew she loved country and so there were touches of it everywhere; even though the rest of his house was sleek and modern; he had even taken the time to use some of her own personal things that she had put on eBay. He must have seen them and purchased them. She was stunned with the amazing thoughtfulness of it.

She finally drifted back to sleep only to wake up shaking and crying; the nightmares had struck with a vengeance.

"It's okay Megan I'm here with you; go back to sleep." James deep familiar voice. He had pulled up a chair and sat with a blanket around his shoulders. He was rubbing her head and holding her hand.

"Thank you" she groggily mumbled and drifted off, this time she awoke to screaming and violently shaking. She was drenched in sweat.

Without asking her permission James crawled in next to her and held her close, when the shaking stopped and he could hear even breathing he knew she was asleep and finally was able to drift off to sleep himself.

Megan awoke the next morning stunned to find James sleeping in bed with her. Mortified she jumped out of bed nearly dumping him out.

"What the?" came his muffled response.

"What are you doing in my bed? How dare you!" She was mad, really mad and he was so bleary eyed from the lack of sleep he was tempted to give it back. The tearful look and the quivering of her chin told him he better keep still.

"Don't you remember anything?"

"No" came the curt reply.

"You were having nightmares. I got in bed so you wouldn't be scared."

Vaguely she remembered the horrible dreams and it was enough for her to realize he was telling her the truth.

His eyes were gently and full of concern. She deserved reproach but instead he blew it off and got up and went without a word to his own room.

Speechless she watched him leave. She felt emptiness without his presence.

"What a way to start things off." She mumbled to herself. She was madder at herself now for the way she had treated him.

She took a long shower relishing the feel of the hot water; without electricity it had been weeks since she had felt anything so good.

She blow dried her hair put on a pair of slacks and a dark green cashmere sweater and her favorite black pumps. The green brought out the dazzling color of her eyes. She hadn't worn make up in weeks and it felt good to have a reason to.

She reached a loving hand to her belly and said "Good morning baby Beth. I can't wait to meet you." She was startled to feel movement beneath her hands.

"James come here quick!" she yelled.

Thinking something was wrong he ran into the room the color drained completely out of his face.

"What's wrong are you hurt?"

"No silly come here I just felt the baby move." She took his hand and placed it on her belly.

"I don't feel…" then a movement beneath his hands brought a startled look to his face followed by a tender smile.

Part of Eric still lived in this new little life and they both shared the profoundness of the moment.

"I miss him so much." He said thinking out loud.

"Me too not a day goes by that I still don't cry." She said through unshed tears.

Before he realized what he was doing he had her in his arms smoothing her hair back and kissing her full on the mouth.

She didn't pull away but surprised him with the intensity of the return kiss. Shocked and embarrassed, she quickly pulled away.

"I'm so sorry James I will never let that happen again. I don't know what came over me."

Something unfathomable shown in his eyes and he quickly changed the subject.

"Are you hungry?"

"Yeah a little."

"Come on down to the kitchen I have breakfast all ready."

It was only when they were seated across from each other at the table that she noticed the deep shadows under his eyes. It made her feel guilty realizing that she was the cause of them. It made her feel even guiltier for the feelings his kiss had stirred in her.

She was still married to Eric in her heart even though he had been dead now for several months. It was all so confusing.

She didn't talk much and James tried to keep the conversation going but she became aloof and almost cold towards him. He sighed; living with Megan was certainly going to be interesting.

They rode together and he filled her in on what the expectations of her new job would be. She was nervous and excited all at the same time.

By the time they got there he had her completely at ease and the old banter of the years of their friendship easily returned.

He introduced her to the class and it was a bit awkward when he introduced her to shocked looks as his wife.

When she realized she no longer was Mrs. Eric Stewart but rather Mrs. James Chandler a wave of nausea suddenly engulfed her and she nearly lost her breakfast in front of them all.

One of the girls came up and helped her to a nearby seat.

"Hi my name's Carly can I get you anything."

There was something that caused Megan to be instantly drawn to this girl, and then right in the middle of one of her most embarrassing moments and at the most inopportune time she heard a gentle whisper in her spirit.

Give this girl your cell number.

She argued with the impression. *No way she will think I am nuts.*

Do it. The impression grew stronger. There was a strange urgency to it.

Megan learned long ago to instantly obey. "Carly I know we don't know each other very well but I would really like to give you my cell number. You can call me anytime day or night okay?"

Carly's eyes widened in surprise but not daring to disobey a teacher she took the offered card with the number on it and stuffed it in her bag. "Yeah, great, uh, thanks."

The rest of the day passed in a blur and Megan found that her long years of friendship with James made him exceptionally easy to work with; she could anticipate what he wanted before he even asked for it.

She found that she loved working with the students and after they got past how strikingly beautiful she was and saw that she was not the least concerned with her looks but totally concerned about them; their apprehension melted and they fell in love with their favorite teachers new wife.

Megan was especially drawn to Carly and although she would never admit that to anyone but James she knew this pretty girl with sadness in her eyes somehow was destined to be in her life.

She kept feeling that inner prompting all day to reach out to Carly which made no sense to her because she had determined not to play favorites and wanted all the kids to be treated the same.

Over and over she found herself talking to Carly, putting her at ease; helping with a complicated problem; a calming hand on her back; an assuring smile. *Why am I so drawn to this girl?*

Love her with all your strength. Feed my lamb.

On the way home Megan was so happily engrossed in talking to James about the day that she didn't notice he was more quiet than usual.

James had kept his eye on Megan all day. He had purposely determined to keep a careful distance letting the students get used to her and establish their own rapport.

Her grace with them only made the knot of longing grow in his heart. She had no clue that she was stunningly beautiful and no clue that her dead husbands best friend was head over heels in love with her.

Guilty pangs assaulted his mind. *What have I got myself into?* He groaned under his breath.

"What'd you say?"

"Huh oh nothing." He was brought abruptly back to the present.

"James there is something going on with Carly."

"What makes you say that?"

"I don't know; it's nothing I can put my finger on just this intuition I get about her." She wasn't about to try to explain to a non-believer that God himself had spoken to her. That would not go over well.

"I'm sure she is fine. She is one of the most popular girls in school everyone likes her."

"There's something wrong James. I know it." She left it at that and decided she was going to do some fervent prayer later that night in the privacy of her room. Times like this she missed the common bond of faith she shared with Eric. They prayed about everything together. It was her turn to sigh.

"Are you all right?" James sensed her withdrawing again.

"Yeah just tired. It's all so much to take in." was the honest reply.

"I know but it's going to be okay we'll get into a pattern you'll see."

She didn't share his calm assurance and she was a jumble of emotions. One minute she wanted to cry the next she wanted to laugh. *Maybe it is just my hormones.* She thought to herself. No it was way more than that and she knew it. Oh so way more than that.

~Lesson Two~

Freedom From the Past

"To all who mourn . . . he will give a crown of beauty for ashes, a joyous blessing instead of mourning, f estive praise instead of despair."
(Isaiah 61:3, NLT)

Nothing Hidden True Freedom
By
Bonnie McPhail

O Lord my heart rejoices.
I sing your praises, for you are mighty
and worthy of praise.
All creation exalts you,
For you O Lord are my redeemer, lover of my soul,
My life and my very being.
You fill my lips with singing
For all that is pure, lovely and of a good report.
I am filled with joy!
This is the song of life that you have given me.
I find in you peace, love, hope, forgiveness.
You bring about all that is good.
I sit at your feet. I listen. I wait.
O Lord I bow in adoration,
Simply for who you are, and for all you have done.
You have made me pure, holy, and clean.
There is nothing hidden from you.
What an incredible freedom in this.
I soar on the wind of your spirit.
You alone are God.

After reading the previous excerpt from the book answer these questions together:

1. Should Christians have nightmares if they are trusting God?

2. What suggestions could you give to help someone who is going through trauma like Megan?

3. Are there any scriptures you can think of that would pertain to this situation?

4. What would you do if you were Megan?

5. What advice would you give a friend going through the same thing?

I have great news for you: God can use all your past experiences—even the most painful ones—to help you grow. In fact, once He breathes new life into them, the "ashes" of our lives can grow to be the strongest trees in our spiritual orchards.

In order to begin the healing process, it is important that we are able to take an honest look at the people or circumstances that have caused us pain.

Take a few moments and write down in your journal what some of the "ashes" of your life have been. These could include past failures, times of deep discouragement, broken relationships, unfulfilled dreams, or wounds inflicted upon you by others.

Write the answers to these questions in your journal:

1. What things have caused you to "mourn" or be in "despair"?

2. List all the people who have caused you pain.

3. What did they do that caused the pain?

4. Write out your true feelings.

5. Choose the one that has hurt you the most and even if they are passed away write them a letter in your journal. Tell them how you feel.

"To all who mourn . . . he will give a crown of beauty for ashes, a joyous blessing instead of mourning, festive praise instead of despair."

(Isaiah 61:3, NLT)

Let's take a look at this verse together. What's amazing about this verse is that God promises to breathe life into the ashes of our lives. Who else could take something that's been destroyed—ground into the dirt, utterly beyond repair—and make something beautiful and new of it?

Let's see what He's promised to give us, in exchange for our ashes. . . .

Answer these questions together:

1. What type of person wears a crown?

   _____

   _____

   _____

   _____

   _____

2. What attributes—character qualities—do we usually envision this person possessing?

   _____

   _____

   _____

   _____

   _____

One definition of a "crown" is an "emblem of glory." An emblem is something that represents something else. So here, the crown represents the glory of the Lord.

"Beauty" can be defined as "the meek, spiritual worship, the Messiah, holy garments and Christian ministries." So, in this context, God is not speaking of physical beauty; rather, He is speaking of the beauty of Himself.

In other words, He will crown us with the glory of Himself. And only He alone can exchange our ashes for this crown of beauty.

We are not expected to do it; in fact, we cannot do it. Can you envision yourself as a crown-wearer? Is it just possible that God's desire is for you to possess all the qualities of royalty, holding

your head up high, rather than wallowing in the

ashes of your past?   This week, ask the Lord to

help you fully grasp this truth.

Prayer

Dear Lord

This week we have talked and shared about the things of our past that have caused us pain. Thank you for revealing what has caused us the greatest pain during our journaling time.

Help us all to forgive those who have hurt us; help us to walk away with new understanding from what we have shared together.

I pray that every woman who goes through this time together will be completely healed and that you will give them supernatural understanding about the circumstances they are dealing with.

We love you Lord and we trust in your great mercy, wisdom and grace.

Amen

~ Hope ~

"I know the ashes you have in your life;
I know the times you have felt
Hopeless, depressed, and weary….
I have heard your cries.
Understand that my mercies
are new every morning;
You have only to ask.
I will turn your mourning into dancing.
Through the misery you have suffered, I will
take all of it and use it for my glory,
To strengthen and enlighten you.
It is my promise
to work all things out for your good.
Let go of the past….
Trust me….
I am well able to do more than you can imagine."
~the Lord~

~Swedish Meatballs~

Ingredients:

- 1 Package frozen meatballs
- 1 pint sour cream
- 1 package Swedish meatball mix
- 1 can mushroom soup
- 1 can milk or water whichever you prefer
- Dash of salt and pepper

Mix all the ingredients and put into crock pot until cooked through or bake in the oven (covered) at 350 degrees for one hour

~ Instructor's Guide Lesson Two ~

Opening Prayer – 10 Minutes

Lesson – 30 Minutes

Work on the question in small groups to be shared with each other later.

Demonstration – 10 minutes demo how to make the meatballs

Recipe Share - 20 minutes:

Copy and share each other's recipes on index cards

Close in Prayer – 5 Minutes

Take prayer requests and close in prayer.

~ Week Three ~

Excerpt From A One Year Bride

Chapter Ten

Carly woke up with the worst headache she had ever had in her life. Her tongue felt thick in her mouth and she could barely swallow. Disoriented she looked around her surroundings trying to process what had happened.

The last thing she remembered were blurry images of sitting at the diner at the truck stop with Adam and then images like a nightmare played out in her mind. What had he done to her?

Flashes of insight followed by understanding came. He had used her she realized the truth of it now but at least it had been quick and selfish not cruel and lasting like what her father did to her. *I can deal with this it's nothing compared to what I have already been through.*

She realized now that she would need to focus all of her energy on survival. Something was wrong terribly wrong and cold stark terror laced its tendrils around her mind threatening to make her retreat into the recesses of her drug induced sleep. *I have to fight this. I have to.*

Willing herself to stay awake she took in her surroundings. She was inside the back of a semi and she was startled to find that there were other girls lying around her all drugged out like she had been.

She counted the bodies around her there were six all together counting herself. The reality of her situation hit her like a punch in the gut and nearly took away her resolve.

Looking at the other girls she was stunned to see that most of them were actually younger than she was; no more than twelve years or so. *Oh my God.* She felt a pity for them rise up and she wanted to get them all out.

She had to put that urge aside if she was going to survive she was going to have to stuff her feelings. That was no problem at all she had learned long ago to switch them off as easily as flicking a light switch. It was her coping mechanism and walking around in a state of nothingness was familiar and as ordinary to her as breathing.

Think Carly, think. She reached around to her pocket and unbelievably he hadn't taken either her cell phone or her credit card. Thank God she had tucked those into her pockets instead of her purse. He must have carelessly pulled her pants down and taken what he wanted quickly so as not to get caught.

She knew it would be a matter of time before someone would most likely remove her clothes again so she would hide the two precious items her ticket to freedom.

There were packing boxes wrapped in plastic piled high. They had been placed near the entrance of the door most likely a ruse to hide the drugged out girls behind them.

She spotted a hole in the floor over in the corner. It was dark over there and she nearly didn't dare go over there she could see roaches skittering about and rat droppings on the floor. That would make it even a better hide out no one else would want to go over there either.

The inside of the truck was unbearably hot and her senses were assaulted with the smell of sweaty bodies and urine. Some of them had peed on themselves. It was disgusting and she nearly lost her dinner.

She could hear traffic noises and other semis going past so she knew they must be traveling on the interstate to God knew where.

As long as the truck was in motion she knew she was relatively safe; better try to sleep off the drugs. She was going to have be alert as she possibly could if she was going to survive.

God if you are real I could use a little help here.

Megan was overcome with a terrible sense of dread. She and James had just arrived home and she was sitting on the sofa with cold lemonade pondering about the lovely weekend she just had with him.

Seeing the look on her face James came over and sat beside her; "What's wrong Megan are you all right?"

Not answering she suddenly grabbed his hand and doubled over in prayer, groaning and crying she was praying like he had never seen anyone do before. He wanted to snatch his hand back but just as he did a powerful surge went up his arm and he felt the most amazing presence.

He had never said a genuine prayer in his life but he found himself suddenly kneeling on the floor in the presence of something holy, something real. He joined his prayers with hers caught up in something he couldn't define but knew nevertheless it was real.

It passed as quickly as it came, looking over at her tear drenched face he saw a radiance and calmness and something else; a determined set to her jaw.

"What just happened?"

"God came James. God came."

Suddenly she got up from her kneeling position and dusted herself off.

"We have to go James we have to go right now."

"What are you talking about we just got home."

"I know but we have to go over to Carly's house. Help me find it James if you don't want to come you don't have to but I'm going. Right now. I'm going right now." She headed towards the doors.

Grabbing his keys and her purse he said; "Okay, okay hold your horses will ya I have to get the address out of my files. I am coming too."

~Lesson Three~

Freedom to Understand

"Simpletons are clothed with foolishness,
but the prudent are crowned with knowledge."
(Proverbs 14:18, NLT)

1. In this week's excerpt from A One Year Bride
    Megan was given the supernatural understanding
    that she needed to pray. Have you ever had that
    happen to you? Discuss it here with the group.

2. How does God speak to you? How do you know it
    is his voice?

The three "crowns of beauty" the Bible mentions are:

- The Crown of Knowledge

- The Crown of Glory and Honor

- The Crown of Everlasting Joy

"To all who mourn . . . he will give a crown of beauty for ashes, a joyous blessing instead of mourning, festive praise instead of despair." (Isaiah 61:3, NLT)

Our scripture from last week (listed above) mentions a crown of beauty the verse this week mentions another crown of beauty; knowledge.

So what is "knowledge"? Is it just an accumulation of facts?

The Bible holds a much broader definition of knowledge. While it includes the dictionary's definition—"to discover, analyze and clarify information"—it also incorporates divine understanding about situations or circumstances.

Let me give you an example:

My son Dan, who is in his mid-twenties, was recently diagnosed with cancer. He had been in Iraq, and the doctor thought that he might have been exposed to carcinogens there which caused the cancer. Dan refused to talk about it. He said he felt as if I were interfering, when I pressed him for medical information.

Initially, I felt hurt by his reaction. (Mothers, of course, always want to shield, protect and help their children—no matter how old the child is.) My dad suggested that I leave Dan alone, and not bring up his health issues. But because I am a registered nurse, and have seen first-hand how devastating cancer can be, this was extremely difficult for me to do.

This was a situation where I needed to put aside my own need for information. I had no other choice but to entrust my son to the Lord's care. So I asked God for His divine understanding—His knowledge—about what to do.

We had everyone we knew praying for him: friends, family, our Bible study groups, church family and coworkers.

Two weeks after the diagnosis, while we were in church, my husband Jeff felt prompted by the Lord to go to the altar and be prayed for in Dan's place, since Dan lived in another state. Jeff said that when the children's pastor touched him, he felt this incredible surge of energy shoot through him.

A few days later, Dan called to tell us that the cancer was completely gone! The doctors were stunned, of course. "This has never happened before—and we don't know what to make of it!" they said.

I learned a huge lesson through all of this. Because the Lord was true to His Word and gave me the crown of knowledge for this situation (and I put aside my own desires and obeyed Him), God was able to perform a miracle.

If I had not asked for divine knowledge, but instead pressed Dan for more medical knowledge, it probably would have alienated my son. I would have driven him away, and it would have created ashes of pain in both of our lives.

Can you think of a time in your own life when the Lord gave you divine understanding about a situation? Take a moment to write about it in your journal.

Are you currently in a situation where you need the Lord to give you His divine understanding—your own crown of knowledge? This goes in the journal too.

Take a moment to pray:

"Dear Lord,

I desperately need the crown of knowledge—Your divine understanding about the situations in my life. By Your Spirit, please reveal hidden things to me. Thank You for promising to give me Your insight; I know that a deeper understanding of these situations will bring healing.

I ask all these things in Jesus' name, Amen."

Close your eyes. What pops into your head? The Lord may bring to mind the name of a trusted friend, a Scripture, or a song. Perhaps a scene may flash through your mind.

Now open your eyes. What did the Lord show you, during this time? Write it down in your journal to ponder and pray about later.

God tells us to meditate on His Word. When we do, He has the opportunity to speak to us on a very personal level. He wants to give you a crown of knowledge—His divine understanding—about every situation in your life.

~Provision~

"How I long to show you My comfort,

My provision, My rest, and My purposes for your life.

Spend time with Me, and I will teach you.

I will guide you.

So many times My children scurry around

with the busyness of their lives.

If they would only come:

Come sit with Me . . .

Come listen . . .

Taste and see that I am good."

~the Lord~

Recipe - Guilt Free Cake

Ingredients:
- ♥ 1 box of vanilla cake mix
- ♥ 1/3 cup apple sauce in place of the oil in the recipe
- ♥ 3 eggs
- ♥ ½ cup water
- ♥ 1 pkg fat free instant white chocolate pudding
- ♥ 1 small container lite cool whip
- ♥ ½ cup shredded coconut

Preheat oven to 350 degrees and mix all ingredients bake according to box directions. Remove cake from oven and mix the pudding according to directions. Poke holes in the cake with a fork and pour the pudding over the hot cake. Let cool. Mix half of the shredded coconut with the cool whip and use to frost the cake, sprinkle remaining coconut, serve chilled.

~ Instructor's Guide Lesson Three ~

Opening Prayer – 10 Minutes

Lesson – 40 Minutes

Work on the question in small groups to be shared with each other later. If you have time there is a great exercise where you take a piece of paper and pin it to each other's back and write uplifting things about the person the paper is pinned too. Later each woman will have fun reading wonderful things about themselves.

Recipe Share - 20 minutes:

> If your group is small enough you might like to make this week's recipe together or bring it in to share with the group.

Close in Prayer – 5 Minutes

> Take prayer requests and close in prayer.

~Week Four~
Excerpt from A One Year Bride

Chapter Thirteen

By the end of the week much had transpired. James shook his head at the wonder of it all.

He and Megan had gone in the middle of the night to pick up Carly and having no place else to go they decided to have her move in with them. Not wanting the sleeping arrangements to be awkward Megan had agreed to bunk with him and Carly took over her old room.

He felt like Carly was going through enough and for now she didn't need to know about the agreement to stay married for a year between him and Megan.

He had to get special permission to have Carly still attend his classes since she was now a guest in his house but given the circumstances the principle readily agreed.

The three of them easily entered into a comfortable daily routine; each morning they would all have breakfast together, Megan insisted on reading a scripture together and since Carly and James both loved her they tolerated it.

Carly had been to court twice once to testify against her father and the other to testify against Artie Roberts. The latter had such a long rap sheet his was done and over within a matter of a few short weeks and serving fifteen years behind bars. Carly had saved countless lives and her testimony cracked the sex trafficking ring the police had been working for years.

Her father however was another story. He had been in intensive care for a few days and then taken to a rehab unit. There was some paralysis that had resulted from his broken neck he was unable to speak or communicate. The courts were in the process of deciding if he was competent to stand trial. Carly had not made any attempts to see him nor did she want to.

Megan and James rode in to work together and Carly took her car. It had been impounded but they had been successful in locating it.

Megan was becoming a true asset in his classroom. She anticipated whatever he needed before he even asked and the students adored her.

Every boy in class had a crush on her and they all sat up straight and listened intently in class trying to impress her. He had never enjoyed such an attentive group of students. The thought of that brought a smile to his face.

After school he graded papers and Megan got dinner. Carly came home and worked on homework. Dinner was his next to favorite time of the day because the three of them sat around the table and laughed and talked. It was the first time in his life he had the semblance of a real family and it was slowly unraveling his resolve not to allow anyone to get this close.

Megan would often spend several hours in Carly's room listening and letting her talk. He would often hear soft crying as Carly poured out all of the years of hurt and abuse.

His most favorite time of the day was when it was bed time and he had Megan all to himself. They still had not consummated the marriage. She had told him in no uncertain terms that she could not be "unequally yoked."

She would not have a real marriage with him unless he shared her faith and he was not about to do that. She had drawn a line in the sand and the only way to cross it was on her terms.

The long years of friendship gave them a comfort with each other that he had never experienced; he could tell her everything and they often got into heated discussions about various topics.

He found her mind challenging and her sharp wit exhilarating and their physical attraction was increasingly becoming a tangible force that both were having a difficult time with.

She was still having the nightmares and he had a habit of drawing her close as soon as she felt his presence she snuggled close and the horrible dreams stopped.

He could get used to this life and he never wanted it to end but there was a nagging sense that one day it would she was too principled to live like this and he knew it.

One day her faith would win and the thought of that only fueled his anger towards God.

Megan loved the new little family she had now. It was a time of mending and healing from the entire trauma she had experienced from the loss of her parents and Eric. She relished in it and she never wanted it to end.

Carly was opening up more and more about what she had experienced and sometimes her pain was so raw that it was palpable and Megan often cried with her.

Carly would often ask Megan to pray for her and one night she gave her the greatest gift of all when she bowed her head and simply gave her heart to the Lord.

The difference was immediate and profound; peace lit her features she said. "Now I understand Mrs. Chandler. God is real."

"Yes he is and he has a plan for your life."

"I always blamed everything on my mother for running away with another drug addict when I was three; and then I blamed my dad for all the horrible things he did to me, but I sinned too. I hated them both. I feel clean Mrs. Chandler really clean."

Megan gave her a hug and from then on they started reading the bible together and doing bible studies. Carly soaked it up like a sponge and her faith was soaring.

Megan confided in her what the agreement was between her and James and also that they had not consummated the marriage and why she could not do that.

They began to earnestly pray together for James salvation. Megan had to trust it to God with all her heart but she knew they were fast approaching a crossroads.

Dread was beginning to fill her heart at the prospect of what she knew she had to do. *I can't do it God not now I just can't* and she put it on the back shelf.

The weeks went by in a blur and Thanksgiving came and went. It was a glorious meal with the four of them sharing in the cooking and laughing and playing board games together.

Megan was great with child by now. The baby was due in four weeks and she was getting uncomfortable and ready to meet her new daughter.

James would lay his head on her belly at night and talk to the baby; her movements always brought a delighted smile to his face. He was gentle and so sincere and she realized with sudden clarity one night that she was totally head over heels in love with him.

She felt an attraction for this man that was chemical and raw and something she had never experiences with Eric. They had been deeply in love and shared the depth of their faith but she had never felt this.

It made it all the harder to do what she knew she was going to have to and it would be soon shortly after the birth of the baby.

"God help me she prayed. Give me strength I can't do this alone."

~Lesson Four~

Freedom to be You

"But we have this treasure in earthen vessels,
that the excellence of the power may be of God and not of us."
2 Corinthians 4:7 (NKJV)

After reading this week's excerpt from A One
Year Bride together take a few moments and
answer these questions:

1. How was Megan being true to herself?

2. What did she do that demonstrated this?

3. What are her strengths?

4. What are her weaknesses?

God has given you "treasures"—skills and abilities—that are uniquely yours to equip you for the plans He has for your life. There is great joy in discovering what your talents are, and using them for the glory of the Lord!

Before starting today's lesson, take a moment and think about what your talents and abilities might be and record the answers to the following questions in your journal:

1. What are you good at?

2. What can you do that brings you joy and fulfillment? Some people find it difficult to pinpoint good things about themselves, or

believe they really don't have any special abilities. If you're one of these people, think of positive things that others have said about you.

3. What do you think are some of your talents and abilities?

4. Write down ten words that best describe your strengths.

5. Write down ten words others have used to describe you.

For this lesson, we are going to take an in-depth look at the parable of the talents, found in Mathew 25:14-29 (NIV).

Jesus begins the parable—the story—with these words:

"[Imagine] a man going on a journey, who called his servants and entrusted his property to them" (verse 14).

The man Jesus described must have been a person of wealth, because he had servants. Before setting out on his journey, the man summoned all these servants and essentially handed over everything he owned.

"Property" does not just mean land; it also includes homes and everything contained in them—furnishings, valuable family heirlooms, cherished memorabilia.

In the biblical time period in which this story took place, "property" likely also included this man's animals, crops, and any means he had to make a living.

By entrusting his property to his servants, then, this man was giving them everything that was valuable and important to him.

"To one he gave five talents of money, to another two talents, and to another one talent, each according to his ability. Then he went on his journey" (verse 15). (Note: In Bible times, a "talent" was worth about $1,000.)

Not only did the man entrust his property to his servants, he also entrusted his money to them. He could have chosen to put the money in the bank, but instead he chose to give it to three servants in whom he recognized promise.

The man must have known these servants well, to recognize what their individual talents were. He did not compare them or try to make them compete against each other; he let each of them function "according to his ability."

In the New Living Translation, verse 14 begins like this: "The Kingdom of Heaven can be illustrated by the story of a man going on a long trip."

Through this parable, then, Jesus is teaching us a Kingdom principle: God has given each of us specific talents and abilities. Like the man in the story, He does not want us to compare our own talents with anyone else's, or try to be what we're not.

Another wonderful truth revealed by this story is that the man recognized the abilities of each of his servants; he did not give them any more than they could handle. The servant who was given one talent was just as valued as the servant who received five.

The story continues:

"The man who had received the five talents went at once and put his money to work and gained five more" (verse 16).

This man did not waste any time. He immediately went out and "put his money to work." He obviously understood his own talents and abilities, allowing him to double the money the master had entrusted to him.

Knowing our own capabilities is so important! In the Kingdom of heaven, the number of talents we possess is not nearly as important as what we do with them. This servant understood this. He was confident enough in his abilities to just jump right in and use those talents—and see what happened!

Let's continue:

"So also, the one with the two talents gained two more" (verse 17).

This servant did the same as the first: he doubled what he was given. He did not sit around pondering how he could compete against the first servant, or wondering what the first servant was doing. He simply went out and did what he knew to do.

"But the man who had received the one talent went off, dug a hole in the ground and hid his master's money" (verse 18).

When we first read this verse, we might think, "What's wrong with that? He was just trying to hide it and keep it safe so no one would steal it."

As we'll soon see, it's clear that the master gave each servant the same instructions: to make the most of his investment. The other two did not waste any time fulfilling these instructions. They went to work immediately, doubling the talents with which they had been entrusted. But this third servant dug a hole and "hid" the money.

If one has to hide something, it implies that it cannot be out in the open. It also implies that this servant was lazy. It's easy to dig a hole and bury something; what takes some effort is using one's abilities to multiply an investment.

Let's see what happens next:

"After a long time the master of those servants returned and settled accounts with them. The man who had received the five talents brought the other five. 'Master,' he said, 'you entrusted me with five talents. See, I have gained five more.' His master replied, 'Well done, good and faithful servant! You have been faithful with a few things;

I will put you in charge of many things. Come and share your master's happiness!' " (verses 19-21).

The first servant could not wait to show his master what he had done. He had such joy! He was rewarded by being put in charge of "many things." In biblical days, this was considered a badge of honor; and it would mean that the servant himself was going to have a much better life from then on.

The man said, "Come and share your master's happiness." Not only was the servant going to be rewarded with a new position of responsibility, he was also going to "share" with his master. This implies a level of equality. The master elevated the servant to the level of his own happiness.

Jesus reveals another important Kingdom principle here: When we use the talents He has given us, and He sees that we can be trusted to be faithful with them, He will give us even more. He will elevate us to places of influence—and it brings Him joy to do it! We will share in the happiness of the Lord.

"The man with the two talents also came. 'Master,' he said, 'you entrusted me with two talents; see, I have gained two more.' His master replied, 'Well done, good and faithful servant! You have been faithful with a few things; I will put you in charge of many things. Come and share your master's happiness!" (verses 22-23).

Notice that the master gives the second servant the same reward as the first, even though he did not produce as much money. The master was impressed that the servant promptly used the talents he had been given, and didn't grumble and compare his more limited resources with that of the first servant.

Another great Kingdom principle here is that we are free to use our own talents and abilities for God's purposes without comparing ourselves to others. The Lord is just as happy with those who make good use of fewer talents, as He is with those who employ more.

"Then the man who had received the one talent came. 'Master,' he said, 'I know that you are a hard man, harvesting where you have not sown and gathering where you have not scattered seed' " (verse 24).

Notice this servant did not jubilantly approach the master like the first two did. He accused the master of being a hard man, who reaped the benefits of others' work.

"So I was afraid and went out and hid your talent in the ground. See, here is what belongs to you" (verse 25).

The servant actually blamed the master for not doing what he should have with the talent that was entrusted to him! The man's fear became his excuse for doing nothing.

"His master replied, 'You wicked, lazy servant! So you knew that I harvest where I have not sown and gather where I have not scattered seed? Well then, you should have put my money on deposit with the bankers, so that when I returned I would have received it back with interest.

Take the talent from him and give it to the one who has the ten talents. For everyone who has will be given more, and he will have an abundance" (verses 26-29).

In this last verse, we discover the most wonderful Kingdom principle of all: If we will faithfully use the talents we've been given, the Lord will give us even more! The blessings will keep flowing, bringing us joy and gladness.

From this parable we've learned that it is important for us not to bury the wonderful talents the Lord has blessed us with, or use fear as an excuse not to exercise them. And, take heart: it is never too late to open our hearts and minds to the wonderful gifts He wants to bestow on us—and the marvelous things He can do through us, to help others.

Please pray this prayer with me:

Dear Lord,

You know the times when I feel so unworthy to do any good thing for You; the times when I am uncertain if it's Your voice leading me, or my own.

Open the eyes of my understanding and show me which talents and abilities You have given me so that I may use them for Your plans and purposes, to bring You glory.

Help me to forgive myself for the times when I have buried my talents and hidden them out of fear.

Thank You that old things are passed away and everything is new—that it's never too late to touch another person's life for You.

Thank You for the talents You have chosen for ME to have. I accept them without comparing myself to anyone else, and I rejoice in my individuality!

I love You, Lord. Amen.

~Wonderfully Made~

You are fearfully and wonderfully made.

Just as I knew you while you were being formed;

So I know you now.

I have good and wonderful plans for your life.

My plans and purposes bring growth;

Mercy, love and provision.

All that you have need of, I will supply.

Seek me with all your heart,

And you will be greatly blessed.

I reward those who diligently seek me."

~ The Lord ~

Spaghetti Pie

Ingredients:

- ♥ 1 pound spaghetti
- ♥ 1 pound ground beef
- ♥ 1 pound provolone cheese
- ♥ 1 pound mozzarella cheese
- ♥ ½ cup parmesan cheese
- ♥ 1 egg
- ♥ Large jar of spaghetti sauce

Preheat oven to 350 degrees, grease bottom of large casserole dish. Cook spaghetti and drain set aside. Brown ground beef drain.

Put half of cooked spaghetti pasta in the bottom of the casserole dish.

Mix the parmesan cheese with the egg and pour over cooked spaghetti, alternate half of the provolone and mozzarella cheeses over the egg/parmesan mixture; repeat with the rest of the noodles and cheese.

Bake uncovered until the cheeses are melted.

Combine cooked beef with spaghetti sauce and pour over melted cheese casserole.

Instructors' Guide Lesson Four

Praise and Prayer – 10 Minutes

Let the women share testimonies and take prayer requests.

Lesson – 15 Minutes

Have the women break into small groups and let them discuss ways in which the Father has spoken to them.

Recipe Share – 30 minutes: this would be a great time to perhaps begin to plan putting the recipes together in a book to give as gifts or as a fund raiser.

Share Time – 20 Minutes

Since this is the last time the women will be together it will be really important for you to bring closure to the group by allowing them to share how it has impacted their lives.

On a personal note I would love to hear from you to see what impact this book had on your group and your own life. There is nothing more priceless than knowing God used you to touch another.

My personal email is: angelcare6@yahoo.com.

Many blessings to you! I know God will richly bless you for being so faithful to lead this group of women. I pray for open doors on your horizon!

Other Books by Bonnie McPhail:

Product Description

<u>Women of Wonder</u> is an eight-week program for women. It can be completed privately or in a group, and includes an instructor's guide. Through the program, you will discover biblical perspectives about your own personality, talents and ministry gifts, as well as lessons about the gifts of the Spirit. It also includes guidelines for women's health and fitness. In addition, W.O.W. includes a beautiful inner healing devotional, and inspirational "Life Songs." This is a must for women of all ages, and is truly life-changing!

Product Description

<u>Angel Songs</u> are a type of "spiritual song" described in the biblical book of Ephesians; inspirational messages of encouragement, hope and love. These beautiful songs will draw you into a closer, more intimate relationship with God.

About the Author

Bonnie McPhail is an artist and published author.

Along with her husband, she has been active in 's women's ministry, praise and worship, and young adult ministry. She also has an associate degree in nursing from the University of New York, has graduated from Rhema Bible Training Center in Pastoral studies and currently is enrolled in Oklahoma Wesleyan University working on a Bachelor's in organizational management and ethics degree.

Bonnie's nursing background gives her insights into women's physical—as well as spiritual and emotional—needs. She has a true heart for people who are hurting and wounded. Bonnie is a speaker and teacher, and is available for women's conferences and workshops.

Bonnie is also a licensed Assembly of God Minister and she is a Pastor to the women she ministers to.

You can check out her website for book and contact information at:www.thefathersmarket.com